METROPOLIS

ALSO BY RISHMA DUNLOP

POETRY

The Body of My Garden
Reading Like a Girl

CHAPBOOKS

The Blue Hour (Art by Suzanne Northcott)
Boundary Bay

DRAMA

The Raj Kumari's Lullaby (Radio Drama)

ANTHOLOGY

Red Silk: An Anthology of South Asian Canadian Women Poets
(Co-edited with Priscila Uppal)

METROPOLIS

Rishma Dunlop

Mansfield Press

Library and Archives Canada Cataloguing in Publication

Dunlop, Rishma, 1956-
    Metropolis / Rishma Dunlop.

Poems.
ISBN 1-894469-24-0

    I. Title.

PS8557.U53995M48 2005   C811'.6   C2005-906333-5

Design: Denis De Klerck
Cover and Author Photo: Joe Paczuski

The publication of *Metropolis*
has been generously supported by
The Canada Council for the Arts
and The Ontario Arts Council.

The Canada Council   Le Conseil des Arts
FOR THE ARTS   DU CANADA
SINCE 1957   DEPUIS 1957

ONTARIO ARTS COUNCIL
CONSEIL DES ARTS DE L'ONTARIO

Mansfield Press Inc.
25 Mansfield Avenue, Toronto, Ontario, Canada M6J 2A9
Publisher: Denis De Klerck
www.mansfieldpress.net

For Italo Costa

For Joe Paczuski

Contents

It is not much to ask. A place, a making,
two towers, a teeming, a genesis, a city.

DENNIS LEE, CIVIL ELEGIES

SEEING

Oh my city, emerald
buried in ravines, coyotes
prowl your meridians.

I am writing from the road.
I had to see clearly
the single world.

I could describe to you
the lemon groves, the beggared streets,
palaces of gold and marble.
All the cities I traveled
to sit in cafés,
to feel the underworld of subways,
to see vanquished cities burned,
men and women cradling the slain,
jilted sweethearts in every theatre,
to know
there is no consolation except in desire,
only the occasional small bird singing,
a temporary clearing of the disorder of things
that flushes the throats of politicians and warriors,
pours a river of poetry through the larynx.

In the city of the future
the world is bandaging its limbs
against wholesale murder,
bombed schoolyards.
From the crazed skulls of highrises,
needle towers on love's black sea,
the wind overturns someone's sail.
The city is a glass book.
Open it with an unflinching hand of
a severed arm. Read the pages
to the lilt of a nightingale.

The sights and fires of
your streets are cleaved
to me. You stand immutable.
Beauty is in the coming home.

What is ordinary is not possible anymore.

Your towers rise in me.
A different wind turns the vane.
What I am waiting for
is just now being born.

In a city ruled by pigeons and doves I began to see that citizens moved mysteriously in the streets as if in a silent movie. I wanted to speak out to them but the world was deafened by the cries of birds. By the flap of wings. I began to imagine voices that tasted of colors and flavors. So you could describe sound to the deaf, a voice that was like vanilla, or orange, a voice that smelled like brandy. I would count the birds in the square at City Hall as if some numerical sequencing would be a code to explain the numbers I have memorized. The phone numbers of the dead. Sometimes I dial those numbers, profess my love to anyone who picks up the receiver. Catalogue of memories in my hands, thickening in spiral notebooks. The city offers me a biography of rain, every vowel beating against its granite heart.

Still Life

Saturday morning. You gift me with
the newspaper in bed.
I read of the capital city of Slovenia
called *Ljubljana*, meaning Beloved.
There they claim poetry as a national disease.
A love city, province of tenderness where they
too have known the thorn of love.

And here you are—your shoulder
propping up the ruined world.
Under the covers, our bodies practice
living as if our city was on fire.
My hands cover you with poems
that assume another life
unbroken.

In our bed ribboned with newsprint
the world is thick with longing.
We put it to our lips and drink.
Your heart in my skull
my mouth thickens pear sweet.

CITY OF MADNESS AND LOVE

In the alleyways of the city
        some seek the deliverance of heroin.
Others sit in bars, lives anaesthetized in the smoke fume of scotch,
nicotine-stained fingers on the highball glass.
Someone is always having a hard time of it.

Everywhere, grim forecasts, the heart worn down.

———————

What then of love,
        of putting things badly
        our fallibility?
Do we believe we will do better next time?

Schopenhauer writes of the *dissatisfied, egotistical state,*
the world as will and representation.
We are terribly agitated.
        No hope in good works.

What then of love, of desire,
        of endless appetite, carnal urgency
        tasting it everywhere
when according to philosophy, life is suffering, death a promised land.

———————

Some days in the city nothing really touches us.
Everything is transparent, black-curtained government cars
cast their shadows along the avenues.

Even in sleep, life is confusion,
petal-strewn sidewalks
ecstatic thoughts, simple phrases, the
mind pushed beyond what it can take.

The worst is the inconsolable.
The insomniac, *soirs volés, nuits blanches,*
     each night exchanged for something
     darker than he imagined.
Nights of screaming.
Of this he speaks to no one.
A man stunned at the power of his own rage.

     ———

Sometimes you don't want to speak to anyone,
the grip of solitude necessary. You buy an espresso
at the Italian coffee shop, speak abruptly to the
man behind the counter. You walk away afraid, believing
harshness is a sin of magnitude.

On the corner of College and Euclid you see a woman
     with a red-stained mouth.
Her hands smell of reproach.
You watch young couples walk hand in hand
     limbs entangled.

You want detachment but there are moments when you want
to stop them, tell them *I have been in love once, like you*
then you feel some divine expression moving through
the gathering of old Calabrian men on the sidewalk.

You notice gold
sunlit scars on a man's forearm,
children playing in the Clinton schoolyard.
You swear there is something euphonious in
doves crying stupidly in the trees.

Small things

Small things keep you safe:
prayers like the Japanese tie to trees,
clasp of your child's hand,
angels at the gates of your city,
schedules of commuter trains.

Until the blasted church,
machete massacres,
rush hour bombs on subways,
carnage that is the failure of love.
Clothed in our convictions,
we feel our brains slip,
in every bone the fossil of murder,
illness we cannot vomit up,
a hurt so fierce it takes more than
all human grief to beat it down.

You see the exact perspective of
loss as a fading pencil study,
loved one's features blur, smudged detail,
clouds of centuries pass over the image,
through cross-hatched strokes
only a wrist in forced memory remains,
a hand caressing.

In the archives of accusations,
vengeance and the unforgiven,
we are nailed together, flying the black
flag of ourselves.

The farmer continues to till his fields.
In the city we awaken, turn off alarm clocks,
drink our coffee, kiss our lovers and children,
begin again at the train stations, at bus stops,
briefcases in hand.

In deafness to political speech
the eye permits change.
You imagine words fit for a newborn.

Touch me. In the burned city,
we have become beautiful.

Love's no secret now.

EPITHALAMIUM

On her daybook flyleaf
                    ink of nostalgia.
On the radio Patsy Cline singing
Crazy for You. Love's adjectives gather
in a suitcase of skin. She keys it shut to avoid
explosions, flesh fragments across
an open city.

Stretch of limousine on the avenue,
past the swank of the Four Seasons Hotel, the Park Hyatt,
Yorkville galleries and imitation trattorias.
On the leather seat, her thighs pinking under her gown
in the heat of afternoon sun. At the cathedral,
something like fear enters her belly.
Trust's affection no longer marks her. On the radio,
Bonny Tyler's gravel-throated *Nothing But a Heartache.*

One brief moment before entering,
smother of white satin, then she is down on her knees,
her pearls striking the stone steps in the fractious daylight.

The image of first love rises
before her, unaltered, perfect.
How she thought they were immortal
and love would be like that, a folded
wing against the erosion of every afternoon.

The doors groan open.
The sun drills its eye through stained glass.
A Chopin prelude temples her, raises her up
to gather, place her skirts in order.

She enters the chapel,
soft staccato of peau-de-soie heels,
calm like a knit bone.

Across the city courtyards,
the clamor of bells,
crows jamming their beaks with the
juice of scorched plums.

THE NEW REPUBLIC

If I speak for the corpses I hold in my hand,
I must praise the madness that put them there,
speak in a human music,
a language that awakens us in
a Republic of Prayer.

Here, there are magicians finding
coins behind our ears,
chalk between my fingers,
graffiti blackboards,
your hands cupping my breasts.

And you, the one who unfurls the banality
of evil, I'll lift your thumbs from my eyelids,
so that I may see the white page upon which
I'll write my poem.

I have saved your kisses
behind my knees,
in the hollow of my clavicle,
a suitcase full of your poems from the time
before your descent, the Gauloise smell of
your stranger's coat.

Here, the poet is voice,
memory of the guillotine,
sounds of erasure and delight.
Kiss my throat until my
belly tightens, prayers fall into the room.
Give me a recitative,
vowels engraved upon my scars,
light written on the roof of my mouth.
Rub my feet with milk.

Requiem of lilacs,
of plain speech.
I write towards your mouth.
Your language sets my hands on fire.

Memory is a cello,
release of birds into darkness.
Death counts the days on our fingers.

When you are done with evil
you will stand at the mouth of hell
                        and reach for me.
When you can no longer cheat death,
I will close your eyes as I promised,
for need has been our covenant,
our common salt at the end of mercy.

I will close your eyes as I promised.
Then I will eat your heart.

MEMORY PALACE

The air above the city is saturated
with prayers. Like the air in
industrial towns and dreams
it's hard to breathe.
Below, an aerial view of the apartment
where we used to make love.
Nightmare demolition site, cement rubble,
explosion of mortar and brick,
gargoyle beheaded.

In memory,
the unfastened blouse,
your hands stroking my hair.
The world seen through a child's snowglobe.
In the yard we make snow angels
rising from where we've lain on our backs,
flying like children, leaving imprints of
wings and gowns.

There is a love which cannot be moved.
It must die in its place and in its time
destroyed together with the building
in which it stands.
It becomes like Cicero's memory palace,
assigned with beauty or ugliness,
dressed up with cloaks or crowns, disfigured
by stains of blood or mud or paint.
And in this way, we will remember.

SANCTUM

Damaged hydrangeas
in your hands.
I saved you once.
You should remember me.

Listen,
someone has been calling my name
all this time.

Darkness, darkness
Be my pillow

Hush little baby
Don't say a word
Papa's gonna buy you
A mockingbird.

What did you think mercy looked like?

AGNUS DEI

City of snow.
The homeless sleep in the square.
A man with long hair tells me his address
with pride: City Hall, Column 5.
Another John Doe is added to the
homeless memorial posted
outside The Church of the Holy Trinity.
In the distance, architecture of mockery,
towers of glass, houses of suburbia.

If we speak for the dead,
let us stand sentinel,
speak in languages not our own,
speak as conductors of human music
that moves us, playing
our spectral bones in dark days,
music that armors us to beggar motion,
quarrying emptiness.

Through the bitter, restless irritations
of our living, stuff the void with eloquence,
fit the writing to the form of passion.

Harvest nothingness with stubborn patience.
In viral days, there is no churchbell,
no wafer on the tongue,
no Guardian Angel of Utopia.

How razor-clean it was supposed to be.
Now, reason confiscated in the corrugated light,
chalice of memories in this net of stormwind,
even your words scatter across ruined avenues,
insuck drawn across the sky where your
                                    cigarette is lit.

Something is spared when you pray,
stripped as you are in your dark kitchen,
back bent at the end of the day, Jove's rage
in the hollow of your throat.
You take the night in your hands.

You who are quick with the tonguing-up
of blame, learn to take it back. Eat your words.
Their venom may be an antidote for what
ails you. If you say *everything is holy*, try
                              to mean what you say.
In the unrelenting labor of every day,
find in the underside, some sense that love has been
curious and noble, humility after fury.

When your eyes have unclouded,
you will see the shine rising off the
edges of things. You will hear a human
breathing, sense something blue, alive,
singing.

Push against the dailiness,
deliberate in your dreams,
your forms of despair.
Find the notes, tender,
that you strain to hear.
Come to this bed,
the open neck,
hand to lip.
Emblazon the mouth
with a lover's kiss,
trying to massacre difference.

Even plenitude is no gift

without knowing the shape of mercy.
The hand I placed on you,

slow declension of muscle,
the imprint of my grip is your history,
my knuckles your pearls.

Currency of aftermath,
premonitions,
something is being spoken.
All we can do for the dead is sing for them.
The songs are lush.
The stars are in you; they can't be extinguished.

Somewhere there are cities
where the gates are never shut and
                                there is no night.
Somewhere there are cities that refuse to burn.

Acqua Alta

On the first day you feel it
        Venezia   overblown, lavish
                        with gondolas and moonlight.

Later, it feels different
                slow chill of rain against city lights

decay of statuary, crumbling of columns and angels,
                                        ravished stone
the weather rubbing everything away.

––––––––––

In this city of masks, pigeons scavenge
                from tourists in the Piazza San Marco.
If you listen carefully, you can hear the whispers of history
                in the Rio di Palazzo,
                from the Doge's prisons, *Prigioni*
                and the inquisitor's rooms in the palace.

You can hear condemned prisoners led to execution
                        across The Bridge of Sighs.

––––––––––

Lovers have come here trying to redeem, and absolve themselves.

––––––––––

Venice is death in stages
                by drowning.

Boats in the crushed canal sink into its sad skin.
The lagoon labors over us, high water lapping at our feet, *acqua alta*,
detritus of plastic and objects, refuse in the wake of the gondola.

We are under the stern gaze of the Angel of Death,
        lashed to the prow, her golden robes flowing.
Her horn calls the dark waters to scour us out.

———————

Last night in your arms I dreamt of the angel,
        her wings outspread, massive, plumage of a showgirl.
Her breath pungent as anise, released the words of our testaments:
        ragged splinters of good and evil, lullabies, confessions,
        incantations, eulogies.
And her wings burned as she left us in a sky gorged with dawn.

———————

In the dark passageways of the Campo San Giacomo dell'Orio
        a dim light leads us into the village.
The traghetto's light blazes. The bell rings out
        from the church of Santa Maria Gloriosa dei Frari.

It rings for us, pulling us under the rising tide.

Asylum Garden

Crows tear open the sky
                underside of black stars and freesia.

Here your forehead is caressed by the hands of rain.

Enter a place where *poetry is made in a bed like love*
                the shape of your eyes goes round my heart

Tangled with the dawn
                where *the earth is blue like an orange*

and we are eating poppies
                abandoned like a century gone.

Dream Sequence When the Moon is Raining

In the end we don't know what we want
until we are ghosts already

these days
when you have let loose your words into the lethal air
your mouth full of failed prayer
you will remember the adulterous heart
                              anonymous hotel rooms
take the wrapper off the bathroom glass
                          bend your head to drink
                          feel the knuckle of solitude

you will smell the stench of testimony
as you build a tiger life
                          hear the noise of your blood

the fevered heart burns
even the grass grieves

the palsied hand will wrench everything back from its pit of darkness
what is ruined, broken off will be restored to you

you will hear the girl in the next apartment
playing Elgar on a rented cello

renunciation so hard to learn
                          becomes ecstasy in the
melancholy music of bone

you will feel affection's gift
the world abundant in harsh light

elsewhere, someone buried up to her armpits
is being stoned to death
elsewhere, the witness tree reaches for us
elsewhere, the same story repeats itself

we are lost in winter's ache
                    this cankered season
undoing the self
a hard road alongside tenderness

What can I offer my heart up to?

small armageddons
in the waters of disremembering
I will lay me down

mercy made of fire
the century burning in the world's noise
I dream of my left side opened
                    my heart removed

la luna piove how the moon rains into
our dreams of gold *sogni d'oro*
starvelings feed from my mouth

in the moments when you ask to be taken
my hand that has passaged you
will open veins of tenderness
my mouth will suck out your demons

on the days when it is all too much to bear
remember the music that leaves you undone
and every lover's name.

INAUGURATIO

... gods of the city reveal their will through the flight of birds

I

The city is in the eye of the blackbird,
Fixed on skyscrapers, bus terminals,
Garbage dumps.
Witness to muffled emergencies
Someone's heart about to stop
Someone about to be delivered
Someone seeking redemption between
A woman's legs.

2

Winged shadows rake the asphalt.
Three crows drift, black motes moving across
The evening-filtered sky to join the flock of
Thousands in the roost of alder trees. Slow flapping
In the sunset, twos and threes in broken ribbons flying
Over the city. They prick the sky into crimson, the vault
Of heaven opening across domes and spires. In their
Homing, grace touches the faded day.

3

The crow is a childhood story, a totem, a fable, a trickster,
An outlaw, an omen. Four and twenty blackbirds baked in a pie.
A dainty dish for a king. Bedtime song of sixpence and
Empire.

4

Lovers. Oneness in the crossing of boundaries.
Bird and lovers are one.

5

Beauty is in the inflections and innuendos.
In the crow's song, the screech of despair.
Call notes of our dark sobbing, the
Cry seeking mother's ear. Mouths
Crying *Mamma*. Sound of dim battalions,
Mouths opened full of charred memory.
Transcendental étude, fugue.
Oracle of exile, rage, fury, hell.

6

In the city's intercession of symbols, the crow
Joins the other watchers, the guardian gazes of
Gargoyles and dark angels and Art Deco muses.
Shell-shocked eyes open into revelation. The crow can
See through the portholes of creation drilled clean
Through the heart, the stars millions of miles away
And the future and the universe.

7

Nightfall. Crows gather to roost. Branches of
Alderwood sag under their communal weight. In sleep
Not a leaf flinches as they perch, black monks hooded
With penitence. Worms burrow into their dreams. The
Immigrants, the refugees, the displaced, the hungry,
                                        the dispossessed,
Dream of crows that could be plucked like fruit,
                              at first sweet and ripe,
Then poison, rotted with bitterness, the taste of exile they
Know so well in this new home where the crows rise again
And again.

8

The crow travels upwards, white turning black,
Black turning white until wings crash into the moon.
The gaping brain begins prayers for enemies. Tiny skulls
Recite last psalms of gardens and serpents and apple tragedies.
A drunken Adam and
                    Eve's spread legs and everything going to hell.

9

The many prayers exhaust us.
We weep with the crows.
Music of weariness slams into the day.
Eardrums burst and deafness numbs us.
The earth and sky are constant.
Everything takes the blame.

10

In green light and euphony, the crows
Gather dead branches, take them back to
Emptiness, entwine the twigs into the limbs
Of a tree with wild, unfailing patience. Until
What was fallen and lost is reborn, ready to take
Its place in the nest.

11

The blackbird is what we know.
Brains in wings and hands.
Lessons of scriptures and physics.
Lucid, inescapable. The mind is an
Old crow seeking universal laws
Wheeling and swarming at
The edge of the world.

12

The crows rise into a gawkish dance, glossy males
Circling the females. They make their way home,
Their wings outstretched in longing, an
Embrace that nails heaven and earth together.

13

Morning rises in full glitter, the crow's beak
Aimed full-target at the heart of the sun. But
The sun brightens and brightens.
Forces us to smell the day, the whale's den of the ocean.
Dried blood turning fragrant. Placental sweetness.
Vaguely familiar. And we stay, survivors with the earth
And sky. Scent of afterbirth in our nostrils.

Open your arms. Fling the emptiness out across
                                        Boundary Road.
Slow dusk. As the blue hour begins
the air will fill with raven wings,
                        thousands of crows
beating a map of sound,
                        moving east over the city.

Breathe this. The birds filling the air
                                with passionate flying.

———————

The birds filling the air with passionate flying.
Wingbeat.   Sound of your heart.   Hurled through with homecoming.

In the lift of their wings feel the one you have loved all the way.
It has worn you through.

Darkling stain of the beloved.

———————

Darkling stain of the beloved.
                        Sooty feathers.
There are more than thirteen ways of looking at a blackbird.

Dark angel. *All angels are terrifying.*
                        Terror and beauty in their singed feathers.

The city sheds the ash of its day, tunes itself
                        to the winds of infinite space.

The long night comes
                        wing after sooty wing.

PSALM

In the city where I live
A man is arrested for abducting and
Butchering a twelve-year-old girl.

Tonight it rains and I walk
On streets that reek
Of rust and pitch.

Petitions to any god are uncertain.
The sky is spread with vast wings of lead.
No oracular assurance from the pulpits.

Still I pray
Words coming like blood on the mouth.
That the sweet taste be taken from the violent thought
That in the birdless hours
The mother and father of the twelve-year-old girl
Will be granted dreamless sleep
That the lachrymal salt of this rain
Will become original milk.

FILM NOIR

At the Gare Centrale
She fingers the blue
Of her Canadian passport.

Wears the shoes she bought
From the *marché aux puces*.

Crimson, strapped at her ankles,
They once belonged to a dancer
With the Moulin Rouge.

At each city limit
A border to be crossed.
Every language a new currency.

At the hotel in Prague
She befriends the night porter.
Tells him secrets,
Intimate stories of her life.

She is conscious of the weight
Of inheritance
The heft of her mother's rubies
Sewn into the hem
Of her skirt.

Insured
She knows there is always
Someone willing to bargain for the past.

In the Madhouse

Pound writes revisions
of *The Pisan Cantos*
on sheets of toilet paper.

In Dante's heaven of love,
in terraces the color of stars,
the city is remade,
in the heart indestructible,
in paradisal jazz,
Jannequin's Renaissance motet
The Song of the Birds.

Before the world was given over to wars,
beloved the hours.

In Arezzo, paintings by Fra Angelico,
altar fragment, Cassandra's tiger eyes,
birds on wires.
No righteous wars.
Every town needs voltage
built under a fat moon.

La beauté
"Beauty is difficult, Yeats,"
said Aubrey Beardsley when Yeats asked
why he drew horrors.

Beauty is difficult.
Over Lethe, dark petals of iron.
Dove sta memora.
La scalza: Io son' la luna
And they have broken my house.

Wind scours the *terzo cielo.*
Her bed-posts are of sapphire,
for this stone giveth sleep.
In Pandora's box
a white moth.

Metropolis

I

She grabs for the world in a cottage of ghosts, tenants a coach house among the restored Victorians, the rose gardens and fountains. Brick walls still dream of hay and horses, the scent of leather harnesses, the soiled gloves of the coachman, carriage of sleep. A lost earring, a midnight slipper.

The city sometimes forgets where she lives. The streets are confused. Air of cinders and flowers, nerves of the boulevards on edge. Parks desert themselves. The address of her future uncertain.

Outside her bedroom, graffiti across the road reads:

Tom Hendry is a rat
Testified against his older brother for murder

Full moon between skyscrapers, the alley becomes a night-river of sound, smashed beer bottles, obscenities screamed by crack dealers and drunks.

2

In the silo of dawn, we are made of nothing that contents us.
Belongings are gathered—spoon, cup, books. Take polished stillness
from the locked church, prayer notes left between stones, language
from the mouth of a still river, the darkest passages of a holy book.

In the empty theatres of the city, small productions are played out.
Rain-slick, sequestered stories of charred roses, bones of mishap. A
star plummets from darkness and a soul is exiled. In the storms of
dreams, the cup of sleep, a doorway haunted by an open hand,
ambulance wail, the coroner's arms.

The town heaves with pacific slumber. In the ghost houses, bedsheets
on furniture, desire is left undone. Any backward glance is fictive.

3

Diaries record the weather as corpses resist the hands of the living. A bullet streams through her hair in a city that is a thousand years shattered place. The streets are strewn with accordioned paper, notebooks of ash. In the coach house, the ghosts of horses tangled in their tethers. She closes a locket, presses parted lovers face to face. Rubs her own image in the mirror until she disappears.

She wants hands for making violins, but for the rest of her life she searches for words that will not come. Amnesia becomes an approach to understanding her life.

She lights a taper at the cathedral. Matinal. Drinks from a bowl polished by the hour lit by milk. The body is light with white lilacs and smoke, morning pearl, ossuary's skull. Terror and beauty in the blue-stoned streets.

4

Humid summer and she remembers love in the fever of other cities—
New Orleans French Quarter rot and filigree, fungal tropic, white cups
of chicory at Café du Monde.

Paris hauntings of St. Sulpice, Delacroix angels, camellias and blown roses.
Lovers in the Jardin du Luxembourg. Ruined gardens weep. The scent of
Billie Holiday's gardenias. In Montparnasse cemetery, Brancusi's sculpture,
stone kiss, *Le Baiser.*

Night smell of lilies. A woman wakes. Releases luna moths among the
stars of constellations. Love is mistaken sometimes. The hardness of
pity bleeds you to the bone.

5

Power blackout. The bride unveiled discovers the bridegroom is a leaky vessel in a blasted marriage.

She tells her lover, *you have come too close.*

In the panic streets, she is determined to live life with her hair flying back like the tail of a race horse.

She does not want love letters. They have no medicinal value. Intimacy is shameful unless it is perfect.

Even in a lover's arms the language of lack. Loneliness which is the truth of things.

6

Citizens work the armatures, bitter locks of anger. She tells her
lover, *I see all the clear cities in you and me, your body coated with silver,
feet chafed by pavements of foreign towns, tongue in a plum.*

Transparent city. Vigil in mortal air. Vodka in the icebox. Their
words like incisions balanced on a bloodaxe. Mother's keepsakes:
child's lock of hair, milk teeth, hospital bracelets.

Morning cool as pearls. Her lover tucks something inside her,
labial secret *memento mori* decree of one perfect thorn.

7

Winter throws its knives against the door. The heat from Sri Lankan restaurants, *masala dosas* and curries muffle the despair in Regent Park.

This city with its esperanto streets, combined tongues and clavicles. Behind each brine-edged argument, a residue of longing. In the ivory towers, academics carry on their lingua franca. The young want a more urgent language, eager to drink, to weep.

Res publica. Surfeit of interpreters all speaking with insistence of a city named Babel.

The man on the corner chants *Sinners will burn forever.* We must be guilty of something. We are doing time on the boulevards. Stumbling to Bethlehem, Mecca, Zion.

8

The city waits, protects itself from Kafka's prophecy in *Arms of the City*. The senselessness of the reaching tower. No absoluteness. That the city would be destroyed by five successive blows from a gigantic fist.

The wind is collapsing the ribs of the chapels, every altar-stone skewed. In the path of resistance, the city doors are locked down. We ride the train to the edge, where the buildings meet the mouth of the harbor. The boxcars slice a path, leave a stiff suture. We hope the train will ease into Union Station, deliver a state of grace, some sacred ground, where all lost things are recovered.

9

At death, two angels stand on either side of you, recording good and bad deeds. You should acknowledge them.

In gunfire streets children are burned instead of fuel. She recites their names. Children of Sharpeville, Sarajevo, Kigali, Beslan, infinite list of cities.

Something turned loose in a child's sorrow. November with graves. Infancy white turns to roan and black. Her words hold the scent of madness as her daughter disappears into a woman. Eyes peer through the windows of ruined houses. Visions of apothecary glass, christening gowns in armoires.

Necropolis. Burnt sorrow in tank-rutted fields. Gangrenous stench. Bed soaked in music.

Scorched we are cherrying the brain.
Gothaming the mind.

At the city's edge   cooling towers.

10

Dirigibles hover in the city's spires. Tattoo artists ink waiting limbs. The woman waits on a subway platform.

This place is not where she began. But here, her body has spilled blood and water, emptying towards the future. Fresh scars are ordained. The city gives her voice, something singular chosen out of chaos.

Memory repeats itself so that the city can exist. Spring batters the mock orange into blossom. Even the trees hunger for music. Someone throws stones on the roof. She practices arpeggios among the bodies in bloody rags, the streets full of cries.

II

The armadas are unleashed into cities and harbors. In the sudden suck of air, she sleeps the sleep of apples. When the city grows down into her eyes, it steals away her infant sight. All history in centuries of bodies, floating in canals, blooming in houses and streets, all flesh hungering, loving, relinquishing, aging, spending itself, the world moving through the corridor of the body, resting sometimes at the vulnerable places, the temples.

Tenderness, our best gesture in the face of death.

12

She notices light in the elms, night kitchens and apartment
bedrooms, in the park, new-hatched birds, the junkie's
delicate fingers. The poem admitted.

In the rose heat of the lung.
The poem that will not hold its tongue.

Refuses to shut its scarlet mouth.

NOTES

SANCTUM—The line "Darkness, darkness be my pillow" is from Jesse Colin Young's song "Darkness, Darkness." *Elephant Mountain*, RCA, 1969.

ASYLUM GARDEN—Italicized lines are from André Breton's poem "On the road to San Romano" and Paul Éluard's poem "The earth is blue like an orange." *Surrealist Love Poems*. Ed. Mary Ann Caws. Chicago: Tate Publishing, 2001, pp. 36, 68.

INAUGURATIO—The poem owes debts to Wallace Stevens' "Thirteen Ways of Looking at a Blackbird" and Ted Hughes' *Crow*. Epigraph adapted from Fustel de Coulanges' *La Cité Antique*, Paris 1880, page 153. The inauguratio was a complex rite to choose the site of a city. Coulanges wrote about the founding of Rome and Romulus: "Being a Latin, a neighbor of the Etruscans and an·initiate in the science of augury, he asked the gods to reveal their will through the flight of birds...."

IN THE MADHOUSE—Italicized lines are from Ezra Pound's *The Pisan Cantos*. Ed. Richard Sieburth. ©1948 Ezra Pound. © 2003 Richard Sieburth. New York: New Directions. Canto 80.

METROPOLIS—Some phrases in sections 6 and 9 are influenced and inspired by my readings of Ann Carson's *Men in the Off Hours*. Toronto: Vintage, 2001.

Acknowledgements

I would like to express my grateful acknowledgement to the Ontario
Arts Council and Toronto Arts Council for grants which supported
the writing of this book.

My thanks to Denis De Klerck for his editing and publishing support.

Thanks to Joe Paczuski and Jason Guriel, for astute readings,
editing suggestions and conversations about these poems.

Some of these poems appeared in *Descant, Poiesis,* and in the limited
edition chapbook *The Blue Hour.*

Thanks to artist Suzanne Northcott for including poems from
Metropolis in an audio sequence in the multimedia installation of her
exhibition *Crossing Boundary,* Surrey Art Gallery, British Columbia,
August 2005. Thanks also to Liane Davison, curator of the gallery.

A selection from this manuscript was part of a lecture titled
"Tenderness in Every Geography: Poetry, Deep Ecology and Humanism"
given at the American Educational Researchers' Association
Conference in Montreal, Quebec in April 2005.

Rishma Dunlop is a poet, dramatist, fiction writer and essayist. She is the author of two previous books of poetry, *The Body of My Garden* and *Reading Like a Girl*. She was a finalist for the CBC Canada Council Award for Poetry in 1998 and winner of The Emily Dickinson Award in 2003. She is a professor of Literary Studies and Arts Education at York University, Toronto.

On the Poetry of Rishma Dunlop

Dunlop's phrasing... can spur leaps of the heart; she's a writer whose passion and large-spiritedness are inspiring.

Barbara Carey, *Toronto Star*

If there is a precipice at which language, especially its lyrical form, must hover, in order for one to feel dangerously alive and subsequently on the verge of death, then Toronto poet Rishma Dunlop takes us there, seducing us with a relentless passion for the intangible beauty wrought visible in 'objects' cathected with reverence and desire.

Lydia Kwa, *West Coast Line*

This is poetry that has the smell of ink and the smell of skin, as Dunlop writes: "a poetry of shine." Dunlop speaks eloquently from the perspective of a witness as much as a participant, bringing us into a world one can't be immune to.

Goran Simic

Lines that startle and please so much you might, like me write them down, think of committing them to memory, wishing they were your own.

Dennis Cooley